GENDER DANGER:

Survivors of Rape, Human Trafficking, and Honor Killings

Survivors: Ordinary People, Extaordinary Circumstances

An Enemy Within:
Overcoming Cancer and Other Life-Threatening Diseases

Danger in the Deep:
Surviving Shark Attacks

Gender Danger:
Survivors of Rape, Human Trafficking, and Honor Killings

In Defense of Our Country:
Survivors of Military Conflict

Lost!
Surviving in the Wilderness

Nature's Wrath:
Surviving Natural Disasters

Never Again:
Survivors of the Holocaust

Students in Danger:
Survivors of School Violence

Survival Skills:
How to Handle Life's Catastrophes

Those Who Remain:
What It Means to Be a Survivor

We Shall All Be Free:
Survivors of Racism

When Danger Hits Home:
Survivors of Domestic Violence

The World Gone Mad:
Surviving Acts of Terrorism

GENDER DANGER:

Survivors of Rape, Human Trafficking, and Honor Killings

Rae Simons
with Joyce Zoldak

 Mason Crest Publishers

GENDER DANGER: Survivors of Rape,
Human Trafficking, and Honor Killings

MASON CREST PUBLISHERS INC.
370 Reed Road
Broomall, Pennsylvania 19008
(866)MCP-BOOK (toll free)
www.masoncrest.com

Because the stories in this series are told by real people, in
some cases names have been changed to protect the privacy
of the individuals.

First Printing
9 8 7 6 5 4 3 2 1
 ISBN 978-1-4222-0449-8 (series)
 ISBN 978-1-4222-1462-6 (series) (pbk.)

     Library of Congress Cataloging-in-Publication Data

Simons, Rae, 1957–
  Gender danger : survivors of rape, human trafficking, and
honor killings / by Rae Simons ; with Joyce Zoldak.
     p. cm. — (Survivors : ordinary people, extraordinary
circumstances)
  Includes bibliographical references and index.
  ISBN 978-1-4222-0451-1 (hardback : alk. paper) — ISBN
978-1-4222-1464-0 (pbk. : alk. paper)
  1. Women—Crimes against. 2. Sex crimes. 3. Women—
Violence against. I. Zoldak, Joyce. II. Title.
  HV6250.4.W65S5395 2009
  362.88082—dc22
                              2008050322

Design by MK Bassett-Harvey.
Produced by Harding House Publishing Service, Inc.
www.hardinghousepages.com
Cover design by Wendy Arakawa.
Printed in The Hashimite Kingdom of Jordan.

CONTENTS

Introduction **6**

1. What Is Gender?
And Why Is It Dangerous? **9**

2. Violence and Vulnerability **39**

3. Sexuality as a Commodity **47**

4. Mutilated Bodies **67**

5. Unacceptable Gender Identities **83**

6. Punished for Her Family's Honor **95**

7. Building a World That's Safer for Women **109**

Further Reading **120**

For More Information **121**

Bibliography **122**

Index **126**

Picture Credits **127**

About the Authors and the Consultant **128**

Introduction

Each of us is confronted with challenges and hardships in our daily lives. Some of us, however, have faced extraordinary challenges and severe adversity. Those who have lived—and often thrived—through affliction, illness, pain, tragedy, cruelty, fear, and even near-death experiences are known as survivors. We have much to learn from survivors and much to admire.

Survivors fascinate us. Notice how many books, movies, and television shows focus on individuals facing—and overcoming—extreme situations. *Robinson Crusoe* is probably the earliest example of this, followed by books like the *Swiss Family Robinson*. Even the old comedy *Gilligan's Island* appealed to this fascination, and today we have everything from the Tom Hanks' movie *Castaway* to the hit reality show *Survivor* and the popular TV show *Lost*.

What is it about survivors that appeals so much to us? Perhaps it's the message of hope they give us. These people have endured extreme challenges—and they've overcome them. They're ordinary people who faced extraordinary situations. And if they can do it, just maybe we can too.

This message is an appropriate one for young adults. After all, adolescence is a time of daily challenges. Change is everywhere in their lives, demanding that they adapt and cope with a constantly shifting reality. Their bodies change in response to increasing levels of sex hormones; their thinking processes change as their brains develop, allowing them to think in more abstract ways; their social lives change as new people and peers become more important. Suddenly, they experience the burning need to form their own identities. At the same time, their emotions are labile and unpredictable. The people they were as children may seem to have

Introduction

disappeared beneath the onslaught of new emotions, thoughts, and sensations. Young adults have to deal with every single one of these changes, all at the same time. Like many of the survivors whose stories are told in this series, adolescents' reality is often a frightening, confusing, and unfamiliar place.

Young adults are in crises that are no less real simply because these are crises we all live through (and most of us survive!) Like all survivors, young adults emerge from their crises transformed; they are not the people they were before. Many of them bear scars they will carry with them for life—and yet these scars can be integrated into their new identities. Scars may even become sources of strength.

In this book series, young adults will have opportunities to learn from individuals faced with tremendous struggles. Each individual has her own story, her own set of circumstances and challenges, and her own way of coping and surviving. Whether facing cancer or abuse, terrorism or natural disaster, genocide or school violence, all the survivors who tell their stories in this series have found the ability and will to carry on despite the trauma. They cope, persevere, persist, and live on as a person changed forever by the ordeal and suffering they endured. They offer hope and wisdom to young adults: if these people can do it, so can they!

These books offer a broad perspective on life and its challenges. They will allow young readers to become more self-aware of the demanding and difficult situations in their own lives—while at the same time becoming more compassionate toward those who have gone through the unthinkable traumas that occur in our world.

— Andrew M. Kleiman, M.D.

Chapter One

WHAT IS GENDER? AND WHY IS IT DANGEROUS?

Baby girls wear pink. Baby boys wear blue. You probably knew that by the time you were in kindergarten. It's one of the earliest ways we pass along a gender identity to the next generation.

Human beings (and all other mammals) generally come in two physical, biological forms: male and female. In the human world, however, various **cultures** have attached a load of meaning and value to something that goes beyond simple sexuality. This is what people refer to as "gender." Male and female are sexual categories—but masculine and feminine refer to the separate concept of gender. This means that it's possible for a female to be masculine, and a male to be feminine.

According to the World Health Organization, "sex" refers to the biological and physi-

cultures: the behaviors, beliefs, and products common to specific groups of people.

Examples of Sex Characteristics

- Women can menstruate while men cannot.
- Men have testicles while women have ovaries.
- Women have breasts that are usually capable of producing milk, while men do not.
- Women have vaginas, while men have penises.
- Men generally have more massive bones than women, while women usually have wide pelvic bones.

ological characteristics that define men and women, while "gender" refers to the socially constructed roles, behaviors, activities, and attributes that a given society considers appropriate for men and women. Aspects of sex don't vary a whole lot between different human societies, but aspects of gender may cover a wide range across different cultures. Sociologist C. Moser put it this way:

Gender is the difference between women and men within the same household and within and between cultures that are socially and culturally constructed and change over time. These differences are reflected in: roles, responsibilities, access to resources, constraints, opportunities, needs, perceptions, views, etc. held by both women and men.

As human beings, we have a need to sort our world into categories. Categorization is

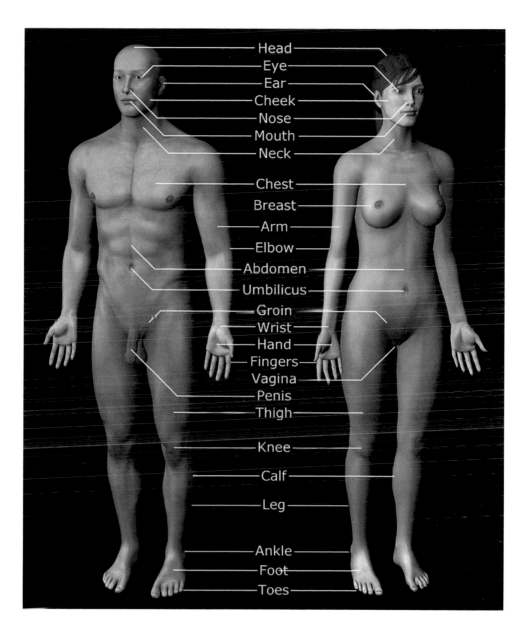

Head
Eye
Ear
Cheek
Nose
Mouth
Neck
Chest
Breast
Arm
Elbow
Abdomen
Umbilicus
Groin
Wrist
Hand
Fingers
Vagina
Penis
Thigh
Knee
Calf
Leg
Ankle
Foot
Toes

one of the basic ways babies make sense of their world as they learn language. As they notice the difference between two things, developing children create a "slot" in their mind where they can put the next thing like

Males and females have basic anatomical differences.

that they encounter. Wake-up time is light, and bedtime is dark; kitties are furry little animals, while doggies are larger furry animals; mommies are girls, and daddies are boys. As adults, though we're probably not aware of what we're doing, we all continue this same process of sorting everything we encounter into categories. The most basic category we use when we meet another human being is gender.

Whether we see someone as masculine or feminine is based on factors that are usually immediately noticeable. Gender is built on four things:

- *Assignment:* The gender we are given at birth, either male or female.
- *Role:* This is the set of behaviors, mannerisms, and other traits that

---

Examples of Gender Characteristics

- In most countries around the world, women earn significantly less money than men do for similar work.
- In North America, dolls are considered appropriate toys for little girls, who are dressed in pink, while little boys (often dressed in blue) are encouraged to play with trucks.

- In Viet Nam, many more men than women smoke, as female smoking has not traditionally been considered appropriate.
- In Saudi Arabia men are allowed to drive cars while women are not.
- In most of the world, women do more housework than men.

The gender of these young adults is immediately recognizable from their clothing and hairstyles.

Although women tend to have less upper-body strength than men, they aren't actually the weaker sex! Physiological tests now suggest that women have a greater tolerance for pain, and statistics reveal that women live longer and are more resistant to many diseases than men are.

society says we should express as part of our assigned gender. (For instance, women may be expected to use softer voices and act more gently, while men can be more boisterous and loud. Or, men may hunt, while women tend the gardens and the children.)

- *Identity:* This is what we ourselves think our gender should be. By the time many people are adults, they do not question their gender. The gender assigned to them by those around them functions as their identity.
- *Attribution:* This is the gender we assign people when we first meet them and is based on a set of cues that are different from culture to culture. (Women may wear dresses while men wear pants; men may have short hair while women have long; women may wear cosmetics, while men have facial hair.)

When it comes to the ongoing process of sorting out their worlds, human beings have a tendency to go beyond the most basic categorization and begin assigning values. Young children add value-laden categories to their mental maps: good and bad, weak and strong, smart and stupid, pretty and ugly. Unfortunately, around the world, young children growing up in many different cultures absorb the message that "feminine" may be pretty, but it is not as good, smart, or strong as "masculine."

THE "WEAKER SEX"

For thousands of years, feminine roles (and the human beings who filled them) have been considered to be inferior to masculine. Feminine people were physically and intellectually weaker. Many cultures even considered them to be morally weaker as well, incapable of the goodness and strength that true men displayed. Women may have been the source of human life, but men seemed to fear and resent this "magic power."

Men saw women as a source of temptation to evil. In the Jewish scriptures, Eve, a woman, is responsible for humanity's fall from perfect unity with God. Greek mythology also blamed a woman—Pandora— for opening the forbidden box that released all humanity's plagues and unhappiness. Early Christian theology reinforced these views: Saint Jerome, a

According to Judeo-Christian tradition, Eve was the one who listened to the Serpent's temptation and then persuaded Adam to eat the forbidden fruit as well. This sixteenth-century painting makes clear that Eve—Woman—is responsible for humanity's fall from perfection into sin.

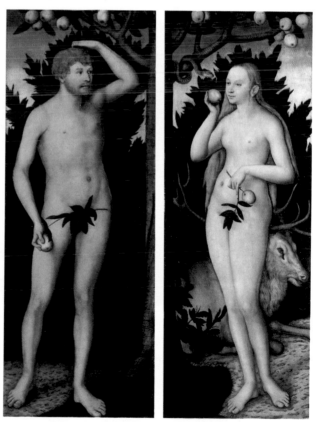

According to Greek legend, Pandora (portrayed here by John William Waterhouse in 1896) was the first woman on earth. The Gods endowed her with many talents, and her name means "all-gifted." Pandora was given a box and told not to open it under any circumstance—but Pandora could not resist her curiosity and opened the box. As a result, all evil (which had been contained in the box) escaped and spread over the Earth. She hurried to close the lid, but it was too late. Only one thing remained at the bottom of the box: hope.

fourth-century father of the Christian church, wrote, "Woman is the gate of the devil, the path of wickedness, the sting of the serpent, in a word a perilous object." Thomas Aquinas, the thirteenth-century Christian theologian, conceded that woman was "created to be man's helpmeet," but he went on to say that woman's only really necessary role is the conception of babies, "since for other purposes men would be better assisted by other men." Hinduism, which evolved in India after about 500 B.C.E., required that women obey men. Women had to walk behind their husbands, women could not own property, and widows could not remarry. In both East and West, male children were preferred over female children.

Around the world, especially in the **West**, women were considered naturally weaker than men; they were assumed to be squeamish, sensitive, and emotional, unable to perform work requiring muscular or intellectual development. In most **preindustrial** societies, women were responsible for all the household chores (caring for children, preparing meals, making and caring for clothes, keeping the home clean), leaving the "heavier" labor that took place outside the house to men. (Even today, in twenty-first-century

West: the western part of the world, in particular North America and Europe.

preindustrial: referring to a society or system that does not rely on industry.

Exceptions to the Rule

Not all ancient cultures had a negative attitude toward the feminine gender. The Celts in Europe, many North American Native societies, and some African tribes valued and respected women, and the gender roles were more equal; in some cases, women even had more power and worth than men.

Women Who Broke Free of Their Gender Limitations

During the Middle Ages, nuns played a key role in the religious and intellectual life of Europe. Whole eras were influenced by women rulers, including England's Queen Elizabeth of England in the sixteenth century, Catherine the Great of Russia in the eighteenth century, and Queen Victoria of England in the nineteenth century.

North America, a recent survey found that women are usually responsible for laundry, childcare, and meal preparation—"indoor" work—while men mow the lawn, take out the garbage, and wash the family vehicles—all "outdoor" chores.)

MOTHERHOOD AND GENDER

The ability to give birth to children is a biological, sexual characteristic—but around the world, it has also been heaped high with a heavy load of gender expectations. The concept that "a woman's place is in the home," has shaped women's identities and rights. Today, contraception gives women greater control over the number of children they will bear, giving them far more options in life.

developing world: countries that are not as technologically or economically advanced.

Despite this change in the biological facts that shape women's lives, gender expectations have not caught up. Especially in the **developing world** (but also in "advanced" societies like North America's), cultural pressures for women to become wives and moth-

For centuries around the world, women have been responsible for caring for the home and preparing food. (This painting was made by Dutch artist Jan Vermeer in the seventeenth century.)

ers still prevent many women from pursuing advanced education or careers. A society's educational system, legal framework, and work opportunities are all important factors that continue to interact with gender. Gender expectations shape these three factors—and once in place, these three factors act as a cage that keep gender roles the same, century after century.

"FEMININE" EDUCATION

Since so many people believed that a woman's place is in the home, it made sense that girls didn't have the same educational needs as boys. In colonial America, for example, girls learned to read and write at special dame schools, but they did not pursue their education once they were old enough to take responsibility for a household. Meanwhile, the boys went on to masters' schools and universities.

By the end of the nineteenth century, however, this was changing in North America. Women's colleges were founded, and women began to be admitted to regular colleges and universities. In 1870, about one-fifth of college and university students were women,

In colonial times, little girls attended "dame schools" along with little boys. These were informal classes, taught by an older woman (often in her home), where young children learned very basic reading, writing, and arithmetic skills. Boys were expected to go on to more rigorous studies, but girls generally did not.

and by 1900, the proportion had increased to more than one-third. Women received 19 percent of all undergraduate college degrees at the beginning of the twentieth century, and by 1984, the figure had shot up to 49 percent. Women were earning 49 percent of all master's degrees as well, and about 33 percent of all doctoral degrees.

Education is one of the most powerful ways to change the shape of a gender expectation. But despite these trends, middle-class girls in Western culture tended to learn from their mothers' example that cooking, cleaning, and caring for children were the behaviors expected of them when they grew up to be adults. Tests still show that the scholastic achievement of girls is higher in the early grades than in high school. And in other parts of the world, especially Africa and Asia, girls still have very limited educational opportunities.

THE LEGAL STATUS OF WOMANHOOD

The myth of women's natural inferiority influenced their status under the law. This has meant that throughout most of history, women generally have had fewer legal rights. Early Roman law described women as children, forever inferior to men. (This is still true in many modern-day African tribes.) Under England's **common law**, an unmarried woman could own property, make a contract,

common law: a system of laws in England based on court decisions rather than on written laws.

or sue and be sued—but a married woman gave up her name, and her property came under her husband's control; in effect, her identity ceased to exist, since she was now "one with her husband." During the early history of the United States, a man literally owned his wife and children as he did his material possessions. If a poor man chose to send his children to the poorhouse, the mother was legally defenseless to object.

Gradually, this began to change. Some communities in both England and the United States modified the common law to allow women to act as lawyers in the courts, to sue for property, and to own property in their own names if their husbands agreed. Equity law, which developed in England, emphasized the principle of equal rights rather than tradition, and the concept spread across the Atlantic to America. Now, a woman could sue her husband. States began changing their laws: Mississippi in 1839, followed by New York in 1848 and Massachusetts in 1854, passed laws allowing married women to own property separate from their husbands.

These may have seemed like enormous windows opening up in women's gender limitations. Countless more **subtle** laws, however, continued to restrict women's lives. Retail stores, for example, were within their legal rights to refuse to issue independent credit cards to married women. Divorced or single women often found it difficult to obtain credit to purchase a house or a car. Sex

subtle: so faint as to be difficult to notice or describe.

THE LADIES OF THE CREATION!

No. I.

THE PARLIAMENTARY FEMALE.

Father of the Family. "COME, DEAR; WE SO SELDOM GO OUT TOGETHER NOW—CAN'T YOU TAKE US ALL TO THE PLAY TO-NIGHT?"
Mistress of the House and M.P. "HOW YOU TALK, CHARLES! DON'T YOU SEE THAT I AM TOO BUSY. I HAVE A COMMITTEE TO-MORROW MOF I HAVE MY SPEECH ON THE GREAT CROCHET QUESTION TO PREPARE FOR THE EVENING."

During the nineteenth century, North American and European societies were forced to accept that women's roles were changing. Notice, however, that this political cartoon disparages women's political ambitions by indicating that the woman is most concerned with issues pertaining to crocheting.

discrimination in the definition of crimes also existed in some areas of the United States: for example, a woman who shot and killed her husband would be accused of homicide, but if a husband shot his wife, it could be termed a "passion shooting," or manslaughter (a lesser crime than homicide). Up until 1968, in Pennsylvania courts required that any woman convicted of a **felony** be sentenced to the maximum punishment prescribed by law. Often women prostitutes were prosecuted although their male customers were allowed to go free.

Until well into the twentieth century, women in Western European countries lived

felony: a serious crime with harsh punishments.

under many of the same legal disabilities as women in the United States. For example, until 1935, married women in England did not have the full right to own property and to enter into contracts. While all this has gradually changed in the Western developed world (allowing changes to gender roles as well), women in many places of the world still lack the same legal protections that men have. In the twentieth century, women in most nations won the right to vote, and this new power allows them more say in the legal structure that encloses their lives.

GENDER AND EMPLOYMENT OPPORTUNITIES

Since wifehood and motherhood were considered women's most important professions, men (who held the authority in many societies) did not want to encourage women to work outside the home. This meant that women had very few ways to support themselves without a man's help. Restricted gender expectations were what brought this

More Exceptions to the Rule

In colonial America, women who needed to support themselves usually became seamstresses or kept boardinghouses—but some women worked in professions and jobs available mostly to men. Colonial America had women doctors, lawyers, preachers, teachers, writers, and singers.

During World War II, with so many men overseas fighting the war, women took over many factory jobs. After the war was over, some women were reluctant to give up their new employment opportunities. They had proved to the world that women could do "men's jobs."

about—and this reality then kept those gender expectations in place.

Gradually, however, the changing reality of the industrial world brought change to gender roles as well. In the nineteenth century, women began working outside their homes in textile mills and garment shops. These new "opportunities" were often a very mixed blessing. In poorly ventilated, crowded rooms women (and children) worked for as long as twelve hours a day. Great Britain passed a ten-hour-day law for women and children in 1847, but in the United States it was not until the 1910s that the states began to pass legislation limiting working hours and improving the working conditions of women and children.

During the 1960s in the United States, several federal laws were passed that improved women's economic status. The Equal Pay Act of 1963 required equal wages for men and women doing equal work. The Civil Rights Act of 1964 prohibited **discrimination** against women by any company with twenty-five or more employees. A Presidential Executive Order in 1967 prohibited **bias** against women in hiring by federal government contractors. Great Britain passed a law in the early 1960s that equalized pay scales for men and women in the British civil service.

As educational opportunities have increased and laws have changed, women have more employment opportunities—but these are still not the same as men's. In 1930,

discrimination: making a distinction for or against a person or group, based on race, religion, or other category.

bias: a preference or inclination, especially one leading to a judgment based on prejudices.

Women and Medicine

Before the 1800s in both the United States and Europe, virtually anyone, male or female, could practice medicine. More women than men practiced obstetrics. Beginning in the nineteenth century, the required educational preparation for the practice of medicine increased, tending to prevent many young women who married early and bore many children, from entering a medical career. Although home nursing was considered a proper female occupation, nursing in hospitals was done almost exclusively by men. The American Medical Association, founded in 1846, barred women from membership. By the 1910s, however, women were attending many leading medical schools, and in 1915 the American Medical Association began to admit women members. In 1890, women constituted about 5 percent of the total doctors in the United States. During the 1980s the proportion was about 17 percent. At the same time the percentage of women doctors was about 19 percent in West Germany and 20 percent in France. In Israel, however, about 32 percent of the total number of doctors and dentists were women.

about 2 percent of all American lawyers and judges were women; in 1989, this number had increased to about 22 percent, a percentage still significantly less than men's numbers in the same field. In 1930, almost no engineers in the United States were women; by 1989, the proportion of women engineers was still only 7.5 percent. Most women who worked were still employed in clerical positions, factory work, retail sales, and service jobs. Secretaries, bookkeepers, and typists accounted for a large portion of women clerical workers. Women in factories often worked as machine operators, assemblers, and inspectors. Many women in service jobs worked as waitresses, cooks, hospital attendants, cleaning women, and hairdressers. Despite the Equal Pay Act of 1963, women in 1970 were paid about 45 percent less than men for the same jobs; in 1988, about 32 percent less.

Women were working—but their jobs were more menial, had less prestige, and earned less money than men's jobs. In 1989, women made up more than 45 percent of employed persons in the United States, but they had only a small share of the decision-making jobs. Although the number of women work-

Women and Teaching

In the United States, teaching children has always been considered an acceptable profession for women. However, men were considered more suitable for teaching older students. In the late 1980s more than twice as many women as men taught in elementary and high schools. In higher education, however, women held only about one-third of the teaching positions, and those who did teach in colleges were concentrated in such fields as education, social service, home economics, nursing, and library science. Only a very small proportion of women college and university teachers were in the physical sciences, engineering, agriculture, and law. Today, most elementary teachers are still female.

ing as managers, officials, and other administrators has been increasing, in 1989 they were outnumbered about 1.5 to 1 by men. Professional women did not get the important assignments and promotions given to their male colleagues.

Working women have often faced discrimination in the work world because employers feared that marriage and childbearing would prevent them from being permanent workers. Since 1960, however, around the world, more and more women with children have been in the work force. This change is especially dramatic for married women with children under age 6: 12 percent worked in 1950, 45 percent in 1980, 57 percent in 1987, and by the twenty-first century, more than two-thirds of women with children are employed.

GENDER AND DISCRIMINATION

Discrimination is illegal in many nations. But the prejudice that lies behind discrimination is not so easily outlawed. No law can control what a person thinks! The world is slowly changing, but the attitudes and beliefs that devalue women are deeply rooted. Often, religion reinforces these attitudes. As a result, discrimination still exists. And in some parts of the world, it is still perfectly legal.

Surveys and other studies from around the world indicate that gender discrimination is alive and well in many countries. A

Despite their increased presence in the workforce, most women still have primary responsibility for housework and family care. In the late 1970s men with an employed wife spent only about 1.4 hours a week more on household tasks than those whose wife was a full-time homemaker.

Prejudice is an attitude, a way of looking at the world. When it turns into action it's called discrimination. Discrimination is when people are treated differently (and unfairly) because they belong to a particular group of people.

Gallup Poll conducted in five Latin American countries (Argentina, Brazil, Colombia, El Salvador and Mexico), for instance, found that half of the respondents believed society favors men over women. In Brazil, only 20 percent of respondents, both men and women, believe that society treats both sexes equally, while more than half of respondents in that country and in Argentina, consider that women and men do not enjoy equal job opportunities. The World Values Survey revealed that most men around the world believe that university education is more important for a boy than for a girl. About two-thirds of the male respondents to the survey in Bangladesh indicated that university education for boys should come first before it is offered to girls, an opinion echoed by one-third or more of male respondents from the Islamic Republic of Iran, Mexico and Uganda. These attitudes also carried over to the work world. More than 80 percent of men in seven countries surveyed in the Middle East and North Africa believe that when jobs are scarce, men have more right to work than women. The same percentage of men in these regions of the world also believe that men make better political leaders than women; many women also accepted this as true: over half of women respondents from Bangladesh, China, Islamic Republic of Iran and Uganda, over one third from Albania and Mexico, and one

out of every five women in the United States do not believe that a woman would make as good a political leader as a man.

The United Nations Development Programme developed the Gender Empowerment Measure (GEM) to measure gender equality in specific areas of economic and political participation in decision-making. The measure includes estimated earned income (an important factor that influences a family member's influence on household

Gender equality is a goal for North American society, but in many cases, it has yet to be achieved. Women's conditions in other parts of the world are even worse.

decisions), the percentage of women working in senior positions and the percentage of women in government leadership roles. Gender empowerment as measured by GEM is lowest in countries in the Middle East and North Africa and South Asia, and highest in industrialized countries, although a wide variation in the numbers shows up across even the same regions.

WHEN DISCRIMINATION TURNS INTO VIOLENCE

Gender-based discrimination is bad enough. It limits the options that about half of all human beings have available to them; it restricts their choices about who they are, what they do, and how they want to live. It takes away their control over their own lives. But when "feminine people" are considered less valuable than "masculine people," this means that they are vulnerable to a range of dangers. Some of these—such as hunger and

"The beating was getting more and more severe. . . . In the beginning it was confined to the house. Gradually, he stopped caring. He slapped me in front of others and continued to threaten me. . . . Every time he beat me it was as if he was trying to test my endurance, to see how much I could take."

—a 27-year-old university graduate from Thailand, as reported to WHO

diseases—may be connected to the poverty that is often the result of fewer educational and employment opportunities. Gender-based violence is another very real danger. According to the World Health Organization (WHO), gender-based violence is a major public health and human rights problem throughout the world. This type of violence is often invisible. It happens behind closed doors, and in many nations, legal systems and cultural norms do not treat it as a crime,

Domestic violence is often rooted in the cultural belief that women are inferior to men, and thus can be considered property.

but as a private family matter. It may be considered a normal part of life. Religious and cultural traditions may even encourage it.

Gender-based violence may be a husband beating his wife because she disobeyed

him—or simply because he's had a bad day. Gender-based violence also shows up in the sex trade, where human beings are treated as commodities. It shows up in the forms of honor killings and sexual mutilations. It may look different in different parts of the world, but it's always based on the same false assumption: one gender is not as valuable as another. So if you belong to that gender, you're in danger, simply because of who you are. You're vulnerable to violence.

Gender-Based Violence Around the World

According to WHO:

- Japan has the lowest percentage of women who have experienced physical violence, while rural Peru has the highest.

- The percentage of women who were physically forced into intercourse (raped) ranged from 4 percent in Serbia and Montenegro to 46 percent in rural Bangladesh and Ethiopia. Nearly one-third of Ethiopian women reported being physically forced by a partner to have sex against their will within the past 12 months. (This high rate of forced sex is particularly alarming in the light of the AIDS epidemic and the difficulty that many women have in protecting themselves from HIV infection.)

"One day he returned home very late. I asked him, 'You are so late . . . where did you go?' He answered, 'I went to the red light zone. Do you have any problems with that?' I started shouting at him and he instantly landed a blow on my right eye. I screamed and he grabbed my hair and dragged me from one room to another while constantly kicking and punching me. He did not calm down at that. . . . He undid his belt and then hit me as much and as long as he wanted. Only those who have been hit with a belt know what it is like."

—a university-educated woman married to a doctor in Bangladesh, as reported to WHO

"Emotional abuse is worse. You can become insane when you are constantly humiliated and told that you are worthless, that you are nothing."

—woman interviewed by WHO in Serbia and Montenegro

Emotional Abuse

WHO has found that emotional abuse can be as devastating as physical abuse. WHO's study included:

- being insulted or made to feel bad about oneself
- being humiliated or belittled in front of others
- being intimidated or scared on purpose (for example by a partner yelling and smashing things)
- being threatened with harm (directly or indirectly in the form of a threat to hurt someone the respondent cared about).

Across all countries, between 20 and 75 percent of women had experienced one or more of these acts.

"My husband slaps me, has sex with me against my will and I have to conform. Before being interviewed I didn't really think about this. I thought this is only natural. This is the way a husband behaves."

—woman interviewed by WHO in Bangladesh

"I tried drinking a washing liquid. . . . I went to the hospital for that and they helped me out. I see these faces, his family's faces all staring at me, giving me the evil eye. Like they thought I should do it. I should die."

—woman interviewed by WHO in Samoa

"So I take a blanket and I spend the night with my children out in the cold because he is hitting me too much and I have to take the kids to stop him hitting them too. I would go up the mountain, and sleep there all night. I've done that more than ten times."

—a woman interviewed by WHO in rural Peru

Chapter Two

VIOLENCE AND VULNERABILITY

In a city in Kenya, armed men broke into the house of a thirty-two-year-old mother of three. They stripped off their clothes, and then they took turns sexually assaulting her. A few days later, the woman came to the Gender Violence Recovery Centre in Nairobi Women's Hospital; her injuries needed treatment. Another woman was treated at the center the next day after three men accosted her on her way home. They threatened her with weapons, dragged her into an isolated area, and raped her. These are just two of the many women and girls throughout Kenya who have suffered sexual violence since political riots raged across the country in late December 2007 and into January 2008.

When political violence erupts in a country, women are often most at risk. Law and order has broken down. People are displaced from their homes. Traditional expectations are sometimes swept away in a tide of rage. "Women fear violence any moment," a woman told a United Nations (UN) worker at one of the many camps that were set up to provide support for those who lost their homes across Kenya.

TERRORIZING THOSE WHO ARE MOST VULNERABLE

According to a UN worker in Kenya,

> Sexual violence is not only occurring as a by-product of the collapse of moral and social order in Kenya brought on by the post-election conflicts. It is also being used as a tool to terrorize families and individuals and [force them out of] the communities in which they live. Whatever the motivation, **perpetrators** are **exploiting** the conflict in order to commit sexual violence with **impunity**.

perpetrators: those who commit offenses or crimes.

exploiting: using to the greatest advantage, often selfishly or unethically.

impunity: being exempt from punishment or harm.

Since the violence began on December 27, 2007, the Nairobi Women's Hospital and the Coast General Hospital in Mombasa have reported a two- to threefold increase in the number of women (and children) seeking treatment for sexual assault. At Nairobi Women's Hospital alone, in a six-week period, more than three hundred women and children have sought treatment for sexual assault.

During Kenya's 2008 political riots, women like this one were particularly vulnerable to violence.

Traditionally, women are responsible for caring for and protecting children. This responsibility makes them more vulnerable during times of political upheaval; they must not only care for their own needs, but for the needs of others as well.

As many as three hundred camps have sprung up during Kenya's crisis, but many of these have no official organization. Government and international humanitarian organizations may not even know they exist, but even in the larger camps where services are being delivered, women and girls have few protections. Men and women sleep under shared tarpaulins or out in the open. Privacy is scarce, and legal protections are nonexistent.

Kenyan officials knew that most survivors were not getting the care they needed following exposure to rape and other forms of sexual violence, but they could not address the problem adequately for a variety of reasons. First of all, even in better times, many Kenyan women, like most women around the world, may not report sexual violence because they are afraid or ashamed. Some Kenyan women may even risk being disowned by their families or communities if they speak out against their attackers. Also, women may simply have no one to tell; during the crisis, especially in the rural areas, there were no doctors, no police officers, no one to help; no formal reporting mechanisms have been established for addressing incidents of sexual violence in the camps. Yet another factor is that women who are struggling to find food and shelter for themselves and their children may feel that sexual assaults are not their most important problem. One Kenyan woman told the UN workers, "In a crisis like this, your first thought is to care for your children, get settled down. You don't even think to report . . . you are trying to figure out how to live."

The need to provide for themselves and their children may also make some women feel compelled to engage in sex in exchange for the resources they need. "We have to feed our children; if we don't [have sex with men], our kids don't eat," explained a displaced woman in one of the Kenyan camps.

Of course Kenya is not the only place where women are faced with these types of gender dangers. The world is full of political turmoil; in other African nations, in the Middle East, and in Latin America, women are struggling to survive. Wherever these situations occur, women are at risk, simply because of their gender.

In the war taking place in the Democratic Republic of Congo, women have been particularly at risk. Rape has been used as a military weapon to subdue entire communities. Hundreds of thousands of women have been raped, often by gangs of man. Pillaging and rape follow each new battle in the war, terrorizing entire communities. Forced to flee their homes, people take whatever they can and walk for miles, hoping to find food and shelter. Meanwhile, the hospitals are full of women whose genitals have been cut with machetes and knives,

Gender Danger and Disease

Rapists don't usually use condoms. Many women who are sexually assaulted contract sexually transmitted diseases.

whose bodies are battered and beaten, whose dignity and security have been robbed.

A doctor who treats these women, Dr. Mukwege, told CNN's Anderson Cooper, "You know, [the women] are in deep pain. But it's not just physical pain. It's psychological pain that you can see. Here at the hospital, we've seen women who've stopped living."

Anneka Van Woudenberg, the senior Congo researcher at Human Rights Watch, add that "rape is now on a daily basis—rape is the norm."

> This is not rape because soldiers have got bored and have nothing to do. It is a way to ensure that communities accept the power and authority of that particular armed group. This is about showing terror. This is about using it as a weapon of war

Wars put women at risk, forcing them to endure violence and hardship. "When everything you count on disappears," one woman from Iraq said, "you dig inside yourself. You do what you have to for your children. You take whatever comes. You hold on. Maybe one day it will end. And when it does, you want to be sure you and your children are still alive. Nothing lasts forever if you can just hold on long enough."

The war in the Congo is the deadliest conflict since World War II. Within the last ten years, more than five million people have died and the numbers keep rising. During 2007, more than 500,000 people were uprooted from their homes.

Chapter Three

SEXUALITY AS A COMMODITY

While political violence was raging through much of Kenya, in another area of the country, thirty-three-year-old Emily Ajwang had lost her husband to an HIV-related disease. He left her with her own case of HIV, five children, and few options.

She told PlusNews:

> I had to look for ways to survive with my children. This place is dry most of the year and the only thing I could do to survive was to wash gold dust for the miners, who can give me something small to push me along. At times I also go into the mines to look for gold. . . . My children do not go to school because they help

Like any good mother, this Kenyan woman does whatever she needs to do to be sure her child has the food and shelter it needs.

me in my small work at the mines. My first two daughters also do what I do for the miners and we are able to collect together what we have. . . . These miners we work for will not give you work unless you allow them to come to your house at night [for sex]. In this area people still believe there is nothing like AIDS. They just think AIDS is TB. People have died here, especially miners, but they believe it is TB or some of them say they are bewitched.

Life is difficult but when you have children, you will do anything to feed them especially the young ones. You know when you know you are sick and the child is also sick, you just want to commit suicide. If it were not for my children, I would commit suicide.

Turning to prostitution is an all-too-common solution for women and girls who have few economic options.

"If my father knew that I do this, he would kill me," a young woman in Kenya told UNICEF workers. "But he does not provide enough for me and my daughter, so I have to do this to make some extra cash." Kenyan men pay her $3 to $8 for sex, she said, while tourists will pay more. "But it is not easy to get tourists. I can't go to the beaches to hunt for tourists because police are always on patrol and they would arrest me."

This young woman just turned fifteen. Her daughter is eleven months old. After she got pregnant, she said, her parents treated her like an outcast. "If I asked for anything, they would ask me to find the man who gave me the baby to buy whatever I needed. They always reminded me that I had let them down in school."

Like many other teenagers in this part of Kenya, peers introduced this young woman to sex-for-cash. "They told me I could earn money easily by simply having sex with men," she said. A report on Kenyan sex tourism revealed that as much as 30 percent of teenagers—as many as 10,000 to 15,000 girls—in some Kenyan coastal areas are involved in sex for cash. Nearly half of the girls began when they were as young as twelve or thirteen.

The study found that one of the reasons this is happening is the gender attitudes of the surrounding society. Seventy-five percent of adults interviewed (including parents) said they thought that girls having sex for money was an acceptable way for families to put food on the table.

This particular young woman, however, is aware that what she is doing is dangerous. "This is not a good life," she admitted to the UNICEF workers. "Sometimes the men treat me badly. Sometimes they refuse to pay me and chase me away. Sometimes they do terrible things to me which I can't even describe.

Many women in Africa must select difficult choices from very few options.

. . . My father has said I should go back to school next year. . . . Once I go back to school, I will forget about this life,"

A COMPLICATED PROBLEM

In many countries, including the United States, the women who make their living this way are perceived as immoral criminals—while the men who use their services seldom face consequences. Women are perceived as making a choice to engage in prostitution. Societies often forget to examine the conditions that create situations where prostitution seems like a **viable** choice for women who have few other options.

viable: workable, practical.

In yet another region of Kenya, for example, along the shores of Lake Victoria, a form of prostitution has become a way to supplement woman fishmongers' income. The women yell themselves hoarse to get the attention of the fishermen and middlemen, who control whether or not the women will have anything to sell that day—but shouting alone is often not enough to get the men's attention.

Nineteen-year-old Lillian Onoka is one of the women who jostle and shout for attention. After her parents died from an AIDS-related illness, she dropped out of school and went to live with her aunt. She told PlusNews, "I do not sell fish but my aunt does, and she brings me along with her. I just help her get the fish without her having to scramble." What Lillian means is that her aunt brings

HIV/AIDS and Gender

Women are especially vulnerable to HIV/AIDS. It's a complicated knot with many strands. One of those strands is women's lack of status; this means that when food is scarce, women and girls often get less food than men do, which makes them more likely to get sick. When they get sick, they probably won't be offered access to health care. They're also denied education, and they struggle to find decent jobs. At the same time, as males die from AIDS and other diseases, women are left to support the households. This in turn means they must care for children, the elderly, and sick family members, while at the same time they have the job of finding food and income for the households. Often they are also treated as the property of males, which means they can be used sexually without consideration for their choices. Or women may turn to the sex trade as their only option for supporting themselves and their families. For instance, in Thailand, rural poverty sends many women to the cities, seeking to earn money for their families; many of these women end up working in the commercial sex trade. This in turn puts them at increased risk for catching HIV/AIDS themselves.

All this puts these women in a high-risk environment for AIDS. It creates an equation that never ends:

Being a Woman + HIV/AIDS = Fewer Choices = Increased Likelihood of AIDS

her as a sexual **inducement** to the fishermen to hand over the best of their catch. Onoka says she is not tied to one fisherman, but will sleep with whoever offers the best deal on any given day. This custom is called *jaboya*: sexual favors granted by fishmongers to fishermen and middlemen in exchange for fish. Fishing is the economic mainstay of this community, and jaboya the only way for fish traders to make a living. Stiff competition for a catch that is often scanty means that older women enlist the help of their younger relatives.

Kennedy Omondi is one of the fishermen in Lillian's community. Although he is married with two children, he told PlusNews that he regularly has sex with young girls in exchange for fish. "I would rather have sex with the young girls they bring to us than have sex with my mother's age-mates," he said. Omondi doesn't worry much about using condoms; he will use a condom if a girl brings one along, but if she doesn't, he

In sub-Sahara Africa, more than a quarter of the population has been directly affected by the HIV epidemic. This means that one of every four people either has HIV/AIDS or has a household member with the disease. Virtually no one in this region of the world is unaffected at least indirectly by HIV. Everyone has a neighbor, a teacher, a friend, or a relative who is sick or dying. Fifty-five percent of all women and girls have HIV/AIDS.

will have unprotected sex. This means that not only are these girls being treated as a commodity—an object that can be bought and sold, bartered over, and exchanged for other goods—but they are also at risk of contracting HIV/AIDS.

Any time some human beings are considered less valuable, less *human* than others, the risk exists for them to be treated as goods. Slavery was based on this principle—and so is prostitution. It's a problem that's not confined to Africa and other parts of the developing world. Treating women as commodities happens around the world, including the United States.

MELISSA'S STORY

"I never thought I'd end up a prostitute," an American woman named Melissa said. "I grew up in a good Christian home, at least that's what my mom always said. She meant we went to Sunday school and church every Sunday, we prayed before we ate meals, we didn't swear. Of course, she never knew what my uncle used to do to my little sister and me when we slept over at his house when my parents went away. But that's another story. Except maybe it got me used to the idea. You know? That I wasn't worth much except for pleasing men with my body."

Melissa agreed to share her story for this book, because, she said, "Kids should understand they're part of the same system where

Melissa believes that a prostitute is a "thing" for sale.

I live. They may have never seen a prostitute, they may think prostitutes are sexy or hinky or dirty, but here's the reality—when you accept that girls are second-rate citizens, you're laying the groundwork for little girls to grow up and become prostitutes."

After Melissa's high school graduation, her parents sent her to a strict Christian college, where she majored in education. "I wanted to be a kindergarten teacher back then. I always liked little kids. But I couldn't handle the college where I was. Everyone was so good. I knew I didn't fit in. I would get depressed, and I couldn't seem to focus on my studies. So I was failing, and my parents were mad at me, and finally, I just left. I'd made up my mind I was going to go to the city and get a job, get out on my own, finally be free. I was going to make friends, find someone who would love me just the way I was, all that stuff girls dream about, you know?

"Well, it didn't turn out quite like that. I got a job at Burger King, but I didn't make enough to pay rent. Eventually, I was sleeping in the street, washing in public restrooms. It was starting to get cold, and I was thinking about going home, telling my parents I was ready to try again. And then I met this guy. At first I thought he was my boyfriend. I thought he was great. He bought me stuff, he took care of me. After a while, I realized he wasn't my boyfriend, he was my pimp. I was pretty stupid, you know." She laughed and shook her head. "It started out he was just kind of 'loaning' me to some friends of his. That's what he said. But eventually even I was smart enough to realize that this guy had a heck of a lot of friends—and he wasn't loaning me, he was selling me. I tried to tell myself it was just work, that lots of people do demeaning things, and that there's nothing wrong with having sex for money. But it's not the sex, at least not from how I look at it. It's that I was a thing, not a person. A chunk of meat for sale to people who didn't care anything about me.

This chart shows that about a quarter of all prostitutes are under 25 years of age.

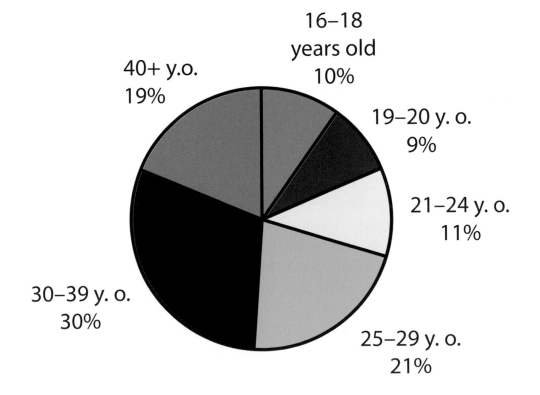

40+ y.o.
19%

16–18
years old
10%

19–20 y. o.
9%

21–24 y. o.
11%

30–39 y. o.
30%

25–29 y. o.
21%

"The first time I got beat up on a job was when I finally realized what I'd turned into. My so-called boyfriend didn't even care. But there was no going back, at least not that I could see then. I couldn't exactly go home after all that, and I couldn't go back to my holier-than-thou college.

"I got sick with all sorts of thing, I'm just lucky I never caught AIDS. One time when I was burning up with a fever, I went into DSS [the Department of Social Services] and tried to go on Welfare. Turned out I couldn't qualify because I needed proof of income for the past twelve months, and of course I didn't exactly have that, did I?"

Melissa is no longer a prostitute, however. She saved her money and enrolled in a community college, and last year she graduated with an associate's degree in computer programming. She has a job she enjoys, and she plans to go back to school eventually to get a degree in teaching. "But I can't see me teaching kindergarten anymore," she said. "I'd like to teach teenagers, maybe in an inner-city school. I think I'm tough enough. And I'd like to teach girls like me that they have options. That they're worth something. That they can respect themselves and work hard and become somebody. That they're not just a body for sale."

Melissa believes education is one way to save other girls from the life she experienced. Education builds self-esteem, she says. It

For young Mexican women like Leticia, life in the United States has represented slavery rather than freedom.

gives women greater economic resources. It shows girls that they have choices.

But some women who become prostitutes never had any choice in the matter at all. Kidnapped or sold by family members, these women are victims of sexual traffic, a crime that spans the globe.

LETICIA'S STORY

Leticia was born in Puebla, Mexico. When she was seven years old, her mother died, leaving her alone with her father. Four years later, when Leticia was eleven, her father gave her as a gift to the local police officer. Raped again and again for the next three years until at last she became pregnant, Leticia lost whatever childhood she had left.

Once her baby was born, Leticia was put out on the street, where she met a man named Aurelio. Aurelio was kind to Leticia, and Leticia believed he loved her. He told her he could get her a job in the United States as a servant for a rich family, but she would need to leave her baby with some of his relatives. With no other options, Leticia agreed—and found herself a prostitute in Tijuana, waiting for a **coyote** who would transport her illegally across the border. She was told that if she didn't go along, her baby would be killed. Leticia did as she was told.

Once in California, Leticia found herself living in a house with other young Mexican girls like herself. A week later, she was being

coyote:
a person who smuggles illegal aliens across the border.

The U.S. border patrol works hard to prevent illegal immigrants from crossing the border. Coyotes rely on often dangerous methods for smuggling people into the United States. People may travel in unventilated shipping containers or be dropped off in desert areas. When human beings are trafficked across the border as goods for sale, their shippers care little if the merchandise doesn't always make it to their destinations.

sold to farm workers for sex. She would often work from eight in the morning until two in the afternoon, having sex with as many as twenty men every hour.

"We are not talking about prostitution alone," said a counselor who worked with Leticia. "What she experienced was slavery. She had no rights, not even over her own body. When a person is forced to submit to sexual exploitation like this, the physical, emotional, and spiritual deterioration is profound." Leticia became physically sick. She turned to drugs and alcohol to cope with the horror of her life.

But something of the little girl who had once known her mother loved her was still alive inside Leticia. One day after her pimp beat her, she found the courage to escape from the farm labor camp. The police found and took her to a shelter for battered women. There she received counseling and began to try to heal. The authorities located her son and returned him to her. Today, she has a special visa granted to victims of sexual trafficking, and she participates in a program designed for child victims of sexual exploitation.

Leticia is only one of thousands of young girls who have been kidnapped or tricked into leaving their homes. Organized crime gangs run a prosperous business off these girls; procurers locate the victims in Mexico, the traffickers bring them to the United

NOT FOR SALE

Phil Marsteller owns a tour company in Brazil that is taking a public stand against sexual trafficking. He states, "I want to fight this cancer that is ruining not only my industry but the lives of those living in the land that I love."

States, and pimps run the sex trade. The girls who are the victims of this trade are poor; they come from families with no money, no resources, no hope. The procurers may build an emotional relationship with the girl and her family, persuading them to let her come to the United States for work (as Leticia was persuaded); or they may simply kidnap the girl—or buy her outright from her family. The procurers often get the girls pregnant, and then threaten to kill the babies as a way to keep the girls from trying to escape.

Sex trafficking is an extreme example of treating women as commodities. It is a widespread problem: experts estimate that more than half a million women are trafficked across international borders each year, and every year 50,000 women are trafficked into the United States. Poverty makes women vulnerable to the sex traffic, as does the cultural attitude that women are commodities.

This attitude can also lead to other violations of women's rights. If women are considered to be merely bodies, objects that can be bought and sold, than those same bodies can be mutilated at the whim of the men in her life.

Chapter Four

MUTILATED
BODIES

When Yin-Lo was five years old, her grandmother broke her toes.

The week before, Yin-Lo had watched her grandmother weave a piece of white fabric. Now the cloth was about a meter long (a little more than a yard). Her grandmother took the material from the loom and carefully cut it into strips.

"Come here," her grandmother said. "Sit down beside me."

Yin-Lo knew her grandmother loved her—and even more important, she knew she had to obey her elders. But Yin-Lo knew what was coming next, and she was frightened. Trembling, she took a seat beside her grandmother.

The old woman removed her granddaughter's shoes. She held one of Yin-Lo's small feet in her gnarled fingers, and then she pushed all the toes backward except for the big toe. At first, Yin-Lo's foot only felt uncomfortable, but then her grandmother began to wrap the strips of white cloth tighter and tighter around her foot, pressing the toes back so that they were folded under her sole. Yin-Lo's toes ached, and she whimpered.

Her grandmother was always kind to Yin-Lo, but now she paid no attention to the little girl's pain. Around and around, she wrapped the strips of cloth, until Yin-Lo's foot looked like a tight little bundle of rags. Then her grandmother picked up Yin-Lo's other foot.

"If you are lucky," she said when she had finished wrapping all the strips of cloth, "you will have lotus of gold feet. Like me." She pointed down at her three-inch long feet (about 7.5 centimeters long). "At the very least you will have silver feet like your mother." Yin-Lo's grandmother held her fingers about four inches apart (about 10 centimeters). "No one in our family has big iron feet."

Yin-Lo sat for a moment looking at her feet. She knew that when she grew up, she would have tiny feet that fit into pretty shoes like those her mother and grandmother wore. Men would admire her feet, and one day her husband would love her more if she could achieve lotus of gold feet.

But right now her feet ached.

As the weeks went by, Yin-Lo's feet hurt more and more. Each day her mother and grandmother sent her outside to push a big

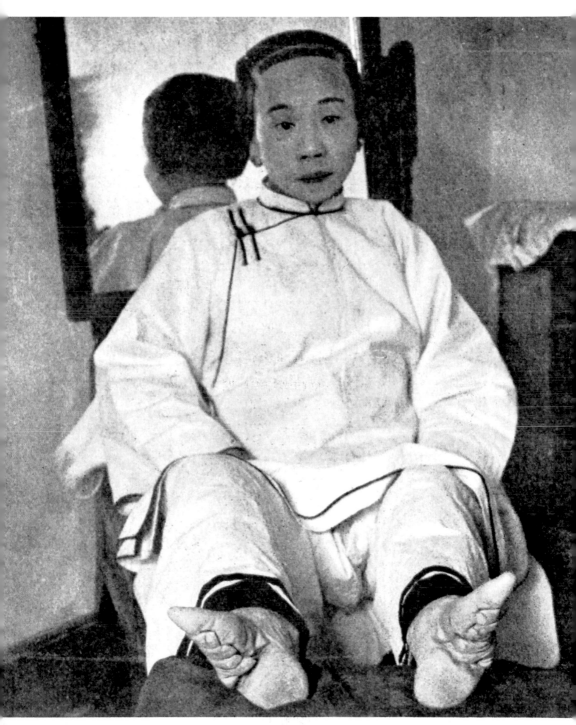

This photograph, taken in 1911, shows a high-class Chinese woman's dainty "lily feet."

Typical shoes
worn by
Chinese women
who had
had their feet
bound.

rock around and around the yard, around and around, again and again, until she wore a hollowed-out path in the earth. "Each step will help shape your foot into a tiny, perfect

Typical shoes worn by Chinese women who had had their feet bound.

cone," her mother said, patting the tears off Yin-Lo's face. "It will make the binding go faster."

Yin-Lo tried to imagine the beautiful red shoes she would wear one day. But each step she took was torture.

Her grandmother would not listen to her cries of pain, and even her mother turned her head away. "It hurts now," she said, "but one day you will be glad. Men do not marry women with big feet."

Yin-Lo's toes felt as though they were on fire. She did not know it, but by now, the tiny bones had all broken. "I'd rather never marry," she muttered.

Her grandmother pressed her lips tight. "A woman who does not marry is nothing."

"A husband will give you sons," Yin-Lo's mother added.

"And when you die, your children will tend your grave," the old woman finished.

Yin-Lo knew how important it was to have someone take care of you once you were dead. When she visited the cemetery with her family, she was afraid of the untended graves, for they were haunted by hungry ghosts, desperate lonely spirits who had no one to care for them. The little girl sighed and bit back the pain that pressed at her lips, trying to come out. She hobbled in another circle around the yard, pushing the heavy stone with her broken toes.

CULTURALLY SANCTIONED TORTURE

X-rays reveal the deformity to the bone structure caused by foot binding.

Yin-Lo belongs to the last generation of Chinese women whose feet were bound. Today, the tradition is no longer practiced— but many generations of women suffered through the same pain that Yin-Lo did.

Footbinding began in China sometime in the tenth century. Although it may have been rare in the tenth, eleventh, and twelfth centuries, by the thirteenth century it was common practice, a practice that endured into the twentieth century. Chinese poets associated bound feet with exquisite beauty. They wrote with wonder of the "slender arcs" small enough to fit in the palm of a man's hand, "moons forever new." Chinese men considered tiny feminine feet to be not only beautiful but erotic; in other words, they were a sexual turn-on.

Many cultures have practices that look strange from those looking in from the outside. For instance, in North America, many women squeeze their feet into tiny pointed shoes that elevate their heels on slender spikes, despite the fact that few women have triangular toes shaped like little elves' feet. In the eighteenth and nineteenth centuries, fashionable women squeezed their waists inside tight corsets; their ribs were compressed so much they could hardly breathe and they often "swooned," but their slender, wasp-like waists conformed to the beauty standards of their day. Styles such as these, like Chinese footbinding, **accentuate** the differences between men and women.

They also serve to restrict women, making them less able to compete in the male world of physical strength. High-heeled shoes affect the way a woman walks and limit her abil-

accentuate: emphasize, stress.

High heels with pointed toes are uncomfortable. They prevent a woman from running or walking on uneven outdoor surfaces. And yet many North Americans consider these shoes to be sexy and attractive.

ity to run; a tight corset impaired a woman's ability to breathe, so she had little energy for strenuous activity; but footbinding went still further. It permanently altered a woman's body. Today, many North American women go through cosmetic surgery, inserting silicon implants in their breasts and sucking fat cells from their thighs—but these body alterations

During the eighteenth and nineteenth centuries, fashion demanded that women constrict their waists to wasplike slenderness. This constriction restricted their ability to breathe normally and may have injured their internal organs.

still do not affect a woman's entire physical being as much as footbinding did. Footbinding permanently changed the very nature of a woman's identity.

A woman who wears high heels to work or for dressy occasions can kick them off when she gets home—but a woman whose feet were bound could never walk normally. She was forced to sit rather than stand; she had to stay at home, inside her house, rather than go out into the world. Because she exercised less, she was smaller, softer, weaker, less energetic. Meanwhile, by comparison, the men in her life appeared larger, more muscular, harder, and more active. Women were languid, delicate, and submissive; men were energetic, strong, and dominant.

Chinese men were attracted to women with bound feet. And Chinese women **internalized** this standard of beauty as well. They shared the perception that tiny feet were beautiful. They took pride in their useless, broken feet, and loving mothers inflicted the practice on their daughters. After all, a good mother wants what is best for her children—and what could be better for a daughter than that she be attractive enough to win a husband?

Other cultures today inflict on women another form of body mutilation: female genital cutting.

internalized: taken in and made a part of one's beliefs or attitudes.

FATIMA'S STORY

"When I was ten years old," said a woman named Fatima, "my grandmother blindfolded me and stripped me naked. I was like a sheep being led to slaughter. Four strong women forced me to lie flat on my back. They held tight to each of my legs. And then my grandmother took a kitchen knife and began to cut me between my legs. I put up a fight, but the cutting didn't stop. The pain was terrible, unbearable."

The procedure left Fatima with severe pain, frequent bleeding, recurring infections, and deep psychological scars. "They told me I was a woman now, that I should be proud. But it hurt too much. I didn't want to be a woman anymore if it had to hurt this bad."

Unfortunately, as awful Fatima's experience sounds to us, it is not a rare one. Around the world, about 135 million girls and women have been genitally cut. Another two million girls a year—6,000 per day—will undergo this procedure.

WHY?

Like footbinding once was, female genital cutting (FGC) is a tradition rooted as deeply in women's cultures as in men's. Young girls often have their genitals cut by the older women who love them best. For these women it is "normal," a necessary rite of passage to

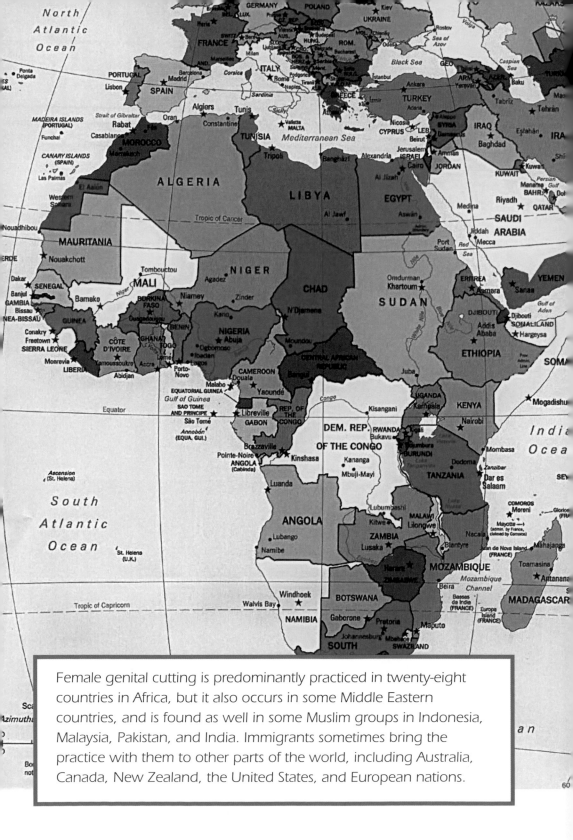

Female genital cutting is predominantly practiced in twenty-eight countries in Africa, but it also occurs in some Middle Eastern countries, and is found as well in some Muslim groups in Indonesia, Malaysia, Pakistan, and India. Immigrants sometimes bring the practice with them to other parts of the world, including Australia, Canada, New Zealand, the United States, and European nations.

60

womanhood. The cutting may be what qualifies a girl for marriage, entitling her to economic and social protection. As with many traditions, people don't think about why they do something; they do it because it's what has always been done, and that very fact makes it seem right.

Sociologists, however, try to understand why certain traditions are rooted in particular societies. Research indicates that FGC, like other mutilations of the female body, is grounded in the premise that males are superior to females. Some reasons men have given for FGC include that it enhances male sexuality; that it curbs female sexual desire (making wives less likely to be unfaithful); that it makes a woman prettier; that it makes a woman cleaner, and less likely to carry diseases; that it makes it easier for women to get pregnant; that it ensures safer childbirths; and that the clitoris is an unhealthy, unattractive, and potentially dangerous organ. Some men argue that FGC has religious significance, but the custom spans religions and is practiced by Muslims, Christians, Jews, and followers of tribal religions alike.

Some women support the practice and

sociologists: scientists who study human society.

The age at which FGC is performed on women and girls varies; it may be performed during infancy, childhood, marriage, or during a first pregnancy, but most typically it is performed on young girls who are between four and twelve years old.

insist that it is no more mutilation than piercing a woman's ears is. For women who have grown up with the tradition, FGC can be an important part of their gender identity. These woman (and their men) may say that the practice must be respected, just as any other cultural tradition should be respected, no matter how strange it may seem to outsiders.

Many women around the world disagree, however. They insist that FGC is a form of violence against women and girls, one whose end result is that a female is subjected to an unnecessary, painful, and dangerous procedure. **Feminists** believe that FGC is a horrifying symptom of the greater problem of gender danger arising from women being considered less valuable than men. The United Nations agrees and has categorized FGC as a violation of a person's right to physical and mental health.

feminists: those who advocate that the social, political, and other rights of women be equal to those of men.

FGC can cause numerous physical complications. Since anesthesia is seldom used, the procedure is extremely painful. Severe bleeding can result, which can lead to shock or death. Unsanitary conditions can cause serious infections, including the spread of HIV. Scarring may result that can interfere with urine flow, causing repeated urinary tract infections. Scarring may also obstruct menstrual flow, which may in turn lead to frequent reproductive tract infections, the inability to conceive children, and chronic pelvic pain.

Taking Action Against FGC

Within the past decade, the silence that has surrounded FGC has faded, and it has become one of the most talked-about subjects among women's groups, especially in Africa. Many communities, governments, and organizations recognize that gender discrimination underlies the practice of FGC and that the most effective strategies for dealing with FGC involve helping women and girls to become educated and empowered within their own communities and cultures. Advocacy by women's groups has placed FGC on the agenda of governments and has contributed to the formation of FGC programs, laws and policies worldwide.

Chapter Five

UNACCEPTABLE GENDER IDENTITIES

C learly, in many cultures females are at risk because of their gender. But what about males who have a feminine identity? Or females who have a masculine identity?

Most cultures are far more tolerant of girls who act like boys than they are of boys who act like girls. "Tomboys" are cute—"sissy boys" aren't. A girl who wears her big brother's jeans and baggy sweatshirts is accepted; a boy who wears his big sister's dresses and makeup is just *weird*. The same cultural rules carry over into adulthood. A "mannish" woman is tolerated, even respected in some situations, while a "femmy" man is looked down on.

According to Michael Kimmel, a sociologist who has studied gender roles, people with **transgender** identities upset those neat

transgender: a person who appears to be, wants to be considered as, or has undergone surgery to become a member of the opposite sex.

little categories we discussed in chapter one. These individuals "show us something that we absolutely, desperately do not want to see: that [gender is] artificial." Transgender people make us uneasy, according to Kimmel.

dichotomy: division into two opposite groups.

continuum: a continuous progression or series, with the parts varying only by tiny degrees.

When your whole worldview is a **dichotomy** between white-black, bad-good, straight-gay and suddenly you see there's a whole **continuum** between them . . . well, this is terrifying to most people. . . . Society responds with confusion and anger. Are you a boy or are you a girl? What are you? You cannot occupy this space. You must choose. You must be one or the other.

This uneasiness may lead to discrimination and prejudice against transgender people. In some cases, it can also lead to violence, even murder. "It's because it's about a kind of rejection of that sexuality," Kimmel told the *New Standard* in a 2003 interview. "It's kind of like purging, not just by murdering something, but by annihilating it; by making it as if it never existed."

According to Kimmel, it is only men who respond with such viciousness to males who identify as women. "We have a very inflexible idea of what masculinity is," Kimmel said. "The violence is an effort to assert that masculinity."

JOANN'S STORY

Joann was born male, but ever since she was very small, she thought of herself as a girl. "No one could accept me the way I was," she said. "Kids my own age were cruel, but the adults weren't that much better. One time when I was about thirteen, a bunch of boys beat me up after school. Another time, I was taking the subway, and some older boys chased me. I was terrified, and I went to the security guard. He just laughed at me. 'You should learn how to fight. Be a man. Stop dressing like that and you'll stop having problems.'"

Joann is an adult now who dresses and acts like a woman; she considers herself a woman, despite her sex. "Some people can accept me now. But there will always be people who can't. It's scary. When you live in the transgender community, you talk about the times you were beat up, the times you got away. You always know someone who was put in the hospital, someone who was killed. People don't know what it's like. If it were anything else—if it were the color of our skin or a disability—people would think it was terrible. But even liberals aren't so comfortable with people like me. We bother people.

"I think it's because sexuality is such a scary thing. And no one's quite as sure of their own gender as they let on. The reality is, I think, that all males are feminine in some ways, all females are masculine—but for the guy who's just a little bit feminine, and he keeps it hidden away deep inside him, someone like me, someone who has embraced my femininity so completely—well, I'm terrifying. He's scared that really he might be not so different than me, and that would mean his

A transgender woman was born male but thinks of herself as a woman.

whole identity was a lie. So he has to reject me. Sometimes a guy like that wants to go further than just reject me, though. He wants to wipe me off the face of the earth. Like I said, it's scary."

Joann isn't exaggerating. According to a report by the National Coalition of Anti-Violence Programs, in 2004, 213 transgender people in fifteen U.S. cities were victims of violence, harassment, and vandalism because of their gender identities. Another report released by the Gender Public Advocacy Coalition (GPAC) indicates that fifty-one people under the age of thirty have been murdered in the United States in the past decade because of their gender non-conformity. The GPAC report included descriptions of each of the victims: Alejandro Lucero, for instance, a twenty-five-year-old Hopi transgender woman, who was strangled and beaten to death in Phoenix, Arizona; and Delilah Corrales, a twenty-three-year-old transgender Latina woman, who was stabbed, beaten, and drowned in the Colorado River.

Mara Keisling, the director of the National Center for Transgender Equality, said that transgender murders are often particularly brutal. "Trans people generally don't get stabbed once," she told *New Standard*. "They get stabbed twenty times, shot, burned and thrown into a dumpster." The GPAC report found that a majority of the victims were killed with violence "beyond that necessary to terminate life." In some cases, assailants continued to bludgeon, stab or shoot the victims even after death. Like Joann said, apparently some men want to completely annihilate transgender individuals.

Most of us don't resort to murder or violence, but gender arouses strong emotional responses in many of us. Homosexuality—where individuals break the gender rules by having sex with members of the same sex—is one of the twenty-first century's most controversial topics in the United States. For many Americans, it is a religious issue; for them, homosexuals and transgenders are not simply different; they are sinful. They have chosen a lifestyle that goes against God's will. Accepting their lifestyles—legally or socially—is often perceived as a threat to "normal" or "Christian" lifestyles.

The United States isn't the only nation facing this issue. Around the world, homosexuals and transgenders face a range of discrimination and mistreatment.

GENDER IN KYRGYZSTAN

Kyrgyzstan is one of the new countries that emerged after the fall of the Soviet Union. Although Soviet laws are no longer in effect in Kyrgyzstan, many of the old attitudes still prevail, including that homosexuals and transgender people are either criminals or mentally ill. "Because male homosexuality was punishable by law, psychiatric treatment appears to have been largely directed against lesbians," one human rights organization reported in the 1990s. "A **pervasive** conviction that homosexuality is indeed a mental

pervasive:
spreading throughout.

We sometimes stereotype transgender people as glamorous cross-dressers, but many more are simply ordinary people. This woman was born as a male and made the decision to have sex-change surgery, allowing her physical identity to match her sense of who she is.

Many people consider a man to be silly or even repulsive if he breaks gender traditions by wearing makeup.

illness . . . provided the conditions for the forced psychiatric treatment of lesbians."

Religion also plays a role in the perception of homosexuals and transgenders in Kyrgyzstan. Mufti Lugmar azhi Guahunov, the leader of the Muslim community in Kyrgyzstan, said in 2005, "I think we should unite

our efforts and maybe start punishing people for such behavior. Thousands of Muslims will be punished by Allah for not preventing, not stopping, lesbians and homosexuals." The Russian Orthodox Church in Kyrgyzstan has also voiced its hostility to homosexuals. Igor Dronov, a senior Russian Orthodox priest in Bishkek, declared that tolerating them "washes out the essence of absolute moral values. Of course, our church will not fight homosexuality with weapons, but we will never tolerate it."

LILA'S STORY

Lila is transgender woman who lives in Turkey. She says transgender people in her country often face violence from the police. Recently, Lila experienced this firsthand.

"I was walking down the street when I heard glass breaking. Some kids had broken a window up ahead. I crossed the street, running a little, because I didn't want to get involved. The next thing I knew, the police were chasing me. They surrounded me, and then they hit me across the shoulders with their batons. They handcuffed me and took me to the police station. Every time I tried to say something, to explain that I hadn't done anything, they hit me again. They yelled insults at me. They kept me overnight, and then the next day, my lawyer was allowed to visit me, and he got me out."

Lila said that in Istanbul, the capital city of Turkey, transgender people are not allowed to even walk past the police stations. "I had a friend who was new in the city, she didn't know, so she was walking along and went past the police station. An officer came out and grabbed her. He punched her in the eye, and then more police officers came out and beat her up. Just because she was walking down the street. Just because she was who she was."

A FINE LINE

You may not feel comfortable around transgender people. For religious reasons, you may believe that alternative sexual lifestyles are wrong. You are entitled to your feelings and to your beliefs. In the United States, our right to believe as we want is protected by the Constitution.

The issue that arises, however, is this: do transgenders and homosexuals also have the right to practice their lifestyles? In the United States, we do not respect child abusers' rights to their "lifestyle," nor would we make room in our communities for someone whose culture required the regular practice of violence. Do gender issues fall in that same sort of category? Are they a threat to the values of our culture? Or do homosexuals and transgenders deserve the same respect and human rights protections as the rest of us?

What do you think?

When it comes to these morally confusing questions, maybe the bottom-line answer is the one that's taught by many religions, sometimes called the Golden Rule: "Treat others the way you want to be treated." In some countries, however, cultural tradition even condones murder based on gender.

Chapter Six

PUNISHED FOR HER FAMILY'S HONOR

hon·or: noun. Good name or public esteem, respect.

When you first meet Amira, you would never guess what she's endured in her life. Her thick hair gleams a coppery red; her dark eyeliner accents her eyes; and her red high-heeled boots match her purse and fingernails, making her seem sophisticated and European. She carries herself with an air of confidence, as though she knows who she is: someone who is intelligent, strong, and beautiful. Amira agreed to share her story for this book, however, and when she did, she revealed how very far she has come.

AMIRA'S STORY

Amira was born in the Middle East to a large family; she had five sisters and three brothers. When she was six, she started school, but at fourteen, when she reached "sexual maturity," she was removed from the school. "I was forbidden to continue studies," she said. "It was time to cook, clean, and then marry."

In the tradition of her community, her brothers would arrange a marriage for her. In all likelihood, they would offer her to the brother of the woman one of them wanted to marry, an exchange that worked out well for the men involved. And so Amira stayed home for two years, waiting for marriage.

And then she met a young man who lived down the road. She was from a richer, more respected family; he was from a poorer one; and yet something drew them together. Although they knew they were breaking the rules of their community, they became friends, and then boyfriend and girlfriend.

They could not see each other openly, so they left letters for each other in the garbage cans outside their houses. Taking out the garbage became a romantic chore for Amira when she would find a message waiting for her. For the next few years, they exchanged letters. During that time, they only spoke to each other once.

And then finally, they risked everything and spent an evening together.

When Amira came home, her family was waiting for her. Her secret had been exposed. They took her to the hospital, where she suffered the indignity of having her hymen checked. Although the doctor confirmed that

Amira stands with her back to the camera to protect her identity.

she was still a virgin, her family refused to believe him until they saw for themselves.

Amira came home from the hospital feeling humiliated and soiled. No one in her family looked at her the same as they had before. She said, "I was looked down upon at home just for going out with him."

Her family punished her by forbidding all the pastimes she enjoyed. She couldn't listen to music; she couldn't leave the house unless her brothers went with her. "I felt helpless and trapped," she said.

Desperate and unhappy, Amira wrote to her boyfriend, telling him she wanted to run away with him. Early in the morning, she crept out of the house, and they took a taxi to a nearby town at the border. But while they sat in a café, they realized that people were staring at them because their clothes were different. Uneasy at the attention they were drawing, they left the café—and found the police waiting for them outside.

"We told the police we were related," Amira said. "We said he was taking me home across the border."

The police questioned them both separately and together. The couple stuck by their story, but when he was threatened, Amira's boyfriend broke down and told the truth. The authorities threw them into a youth prison, where they remained for three months. "Sometimes," Amira recalled, "if the guards were kind, we met for a few minutes here and there in the prison."

Meanwhile, a compromise had been reached between Amira's family and her boyfriend's: her brother raped her boyfriend's mother as a kind of revenge or "compensation." For both families, this seemed only fair. The boyfriend's family had brought dishonor to Amira's family, and now they too must be dishonored.

When Amira and her boyfriend were released from the prison, she was terrified to go home. Both families, however, had signed an agreement that they would not harm either of the young people. Amira did not believe they would keep their promise; she begged the authorities not to force her to go home with her family.

Her boyfriend's family convinced him that if the couple came to them, they would be safe. "His uncle swore to the Koran we wouldn't be harmed," Amira said. "I didn't believe any of them though."

The two young people went to the uncle's house. There they were married and given a small room to share. They stayed there together for nineteen days, too afraid to leave. They had heard that both families hated them now.

Amira's new brother-in-law came to their room and asked to see the blood from the wedding night that would prove she had been a virgin. Her husband refused. "You have no right to see that," he told his brother.

A few days later, the brother returned and said he had a house where they could stay. The couple took a taxi to an empty house, where they stayed for another four or five nights, still too afraid to venture out. The brother returned, warning them that they should move to the country where they would be safer from Amira's family. When the couple was reluctant to leave, the brother pulled a gun and forced them out of the house.

Once in the country, the couple tried again to build a life together. After only a few days, Amira's brother found them—but he reassured Amira that her family had forgiven her. What's more, he had found a job for her husband as a shepherd.

Once Amira's husband was gone to his new job, her brother told her that her family wanted her to come home. "I was ecstatic," Amira said, "but I wanted to wait for my husband to come home from work. My brother refused. He took me by force back to town. Meanwhile, my older brother was waiting at the house for my husband to come home from work."

Back in town, Amira was locked out of the house, penned in the yard for several days like an animal. During this time, she overheard what her brother had done: he had shot her husband seventeen times and killed him.

"They left the gate open one day, and I escaped. I ran to the youth prison and told them what had happened. They took me in. They took me to a woman's protection center. My husband and I had only had a few days together as husband and wife. That was all we would ever have."

Amira spent the next months hiding in the women's center. When her family found out where she was, she moved to a more secure center, where she would be safe from them. Because her family and her husband's had once more reached a compromise: they would each give up a child in the name of

Amira still wears her wedding ring. She wonders if she could ever love another man as much as she loved her husband.

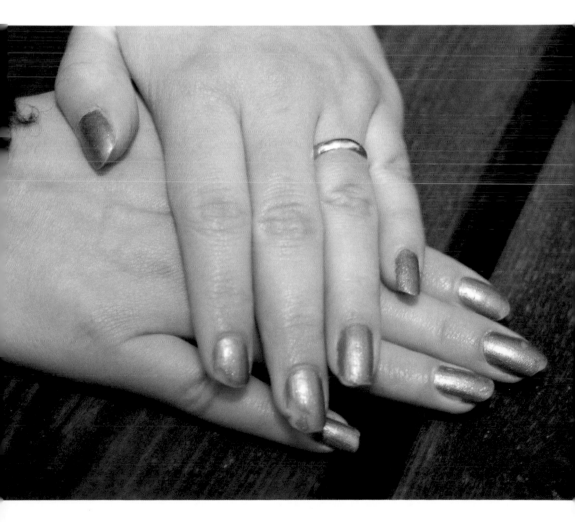

their honor. Her brothers had killed her husband, and now his brothers would kill her.

"My life was always in danger," Amira said. "I felt hopeless. I had to leave the country. I had no other choice." A worker from an international organization helped her to get a passport, a visa, an airplane ticket, everything she needed to escape the country. "When they told me I was actually leaving, I laughed at them. I didn't think it was possible." But it was. Finally, after three years in hiding, she had escaped.

When she landed in the European country that has been her home for the past three years, she heaved a great sigh of relief. "For the first time, I felt hope and freedom, and I smiled."

Amira was completely alone, though, unable to even speak the language of the country that would now be her home. "There is a very different way of life here," she explained. It was hard for her to make friends, and she withdrew into herself. "In the shelter I was always hoping to get out, but once I was out and actually free, I still haven't escaped it. The more time goes, the more I go back to the problems I have. The problem is still alive and becomes bigger and more alive, clearer, even. It becomes clearer every year. I do not forget. It comes back as I get older."

Someday, though, Amira hopes she will once more have a family of her own, someone who will love her, whom she will love. "But," she said, "I never will fall in love as I did. Nobody can take his place for me. I will never forget him."

Although her mother and sisters played their part in all that happened to her, she has forgiven them, and they communicate with each other now. "They have forgiven me too," she said. "Their situation is just as dangerous as mine was. I understand that. And now my sisters envy me because I am free, while they will be forced into marriage." She is glad to be in touch with them once again, but she knows she can never go home. "As long as my brothers are alive, there will be no real reconciliation."

Despite everything that happened, Amira still loves her father—but she hates the way her culture treats women. She knows she is lucky to be alive.

"While I was in the woman's shelter I tried to commit suicide by taking pills. I was saved. But I was taught that suicide was the thing I should do. Suicide is a great problem in my country, and arranged suicides are common. No one investigates them. You are forced to kill yourself for the honor of your family."

When Amira told her story, she was in school, studying language. She wanted to get a job one day working with women. "I want to help people who are where I have been," she said.

A woman from Afghanistan wears the traditional burkha that hides her from all eyes but her husband's. Honor killings are common among fundamentalist Muslims.

HONOR KILLINGS

Each year, thousands of women are murdered by their families in the name of honor. Reports submitted to the United Nations Commission on Human Rights indicate that honor killings have occurred in Bangladesh, Great Britain, Brazil, Ecuador, Egypt, India, Israel, Italy, Jordan, Pakistan, Morocco, Sweden, Turkey, and Uganda; the practice was also condoned under the rule of the **fundamentalist** Taliban government in Afghanistan, and it has been reported in Iraq and Iran.

"In countries where Islam is practiced, they're called honor killings," Widney Brown, advocacy director for Human Rights Watch, told *National Geographic*, "but dowry deaths and so-called crimes of passion have a similar dynamic in that the women are killed by male family members and the crimes are perceived as excusable or understandable." According to UNICEF, more than five thousand brides in India die each year because their husbands' families do not consider their **dowries** to be big enough.

This sort of violence against women occurs in cultures where women are considered property. It's supported by the belief that violence against family members is a family matter, rather than a judicial issue. "Females in the family—mothers, mothers-in-law, sisters, and cousins—frequently support the attacks. It's a community mentality,"

fundamentalist: rigid belief in a set of ideas or principles, often religious and often involving intolerance of differing views.

dowries: money, goods, or land given by women to their husbands at marriage.

Teenage brothers are frequently the ones the family picks to commit the murder because, as minors, they would be subject to considerably lighter sentencing if there is legal action.

said Zaynab Nawaz, a program assistant for women's human rights at Amnesty International. "Women are considered the property of the males in their family irrespective of their class, ethnic, or religious group. The owner of the property has the right to decide its fate."

Honor killings are meted out for a wide range of offenses that include adultery, premarital sex, flirting, or even failing to serve a meal on time. Amnesty International reported a case in which a husband murdered his wife based merely on a dream that she had betrayed him. In Turkey, a young woman's family cut her throat in the town square because someone had dedicated a love song to her on the radio. Even rape victims can be deemed deserving of death; when a sixteen-year-old girl with mental retardation was raped in Pakistan, her family turned her over to her tribe's judicial council. The crime was also reported to the police, and the perpetrator was arrested—but the council decided the girl had brought shame to her tribe and put her to death.

Officials often claim that nothing can be done to put an end to these deaths because honor killing is so deeply rooted in the cultures where it is practiced. Some say the concept of women's rights is not culturally **relevant** to **patriarchal** societies.

How do we know where to draw the line when it comes to respecting the practices of another culture or religion? The United Nations (UN) and other international agencies have worked to define the answers to questions like this—and they are working to insist that women have the right to basic human rights, no matter what their culture.

relevant:
having to do with the matter at hand.

patriarchal:
related to a society in which the male is the head of the family.

Chapter Seven

BUILDING A WORLD THAT'S SAFER FOR WOMEN

The United Nations has launched a campaign to end violence against women and girls. "Violence against women and girls makes its hideous imprint on every continent, country and culture," said UN Secretary-General Ban Ki-moon.

It is time to focus on the concrete actions that all of us can and must take to prevent and eliminate this **scourge**—Member States, the United Nations family, civil society and individuals—women and men. It is time to break through the walls of silence, and make legal **norms** a reality in women's lives.

scourge:
a cause of affliction or trouble.

norms:
typical standards.

The campaign is working to change public opinion and engage the support of top policy makers in countries around the world. It has enlisted the help of private and public agencies to achieve its goals.

The World Health Organization (WHO) has created a list of recommendations that will make the world safer for women. Some of these recommendations include:

Promote gender equality and women's human rights. Violence against women is an extreme **manifestation** of gender inequality that needs to be addressed urgently, as such violence in turn **perpetuates** this inequality. The unequal status of women is also associated in a variety of ways with domestic violence and with women's responses to that violence. Improving women's legal and **socioeconomic** status is likely to be, in the long term, a key intervention in reducing women's vulnerability to violence. This includes: awareness of their rights, and measures to ensure women's rights related to owning and disposing of property and assets, access to divorce and child custody following separation. Women's access to education—in particular keeping girls enrolled through secondary education—and to safe and gainful employment should also be strongly supported as part of overall anti-violence efforts. National efforts to

manifestation: an indication of the existence of something.

perpetuates: causes to continue.

socio-economic: relating to both social and economic factors.

The World Health Organization—WHO—handles all health issues within the United Nations. It is responsible for providing leadership on global health matters, shaping the health research agenda, setting norms and standards, articulating evidence-based policy options, providing technical support to countries, and monitoring and assessing health trends. It lists the following five points as its main agenda:

1. Promoting development in nations around the world in order to build communities with the financial resources to support good health.

2. Fostering health security by providing preventative and protective medication against epidemics and other disease.

3. Strengthening health systems in developing nations.

4. Harnessing research, information, and evidence in order to set priorities and build for the future.

5. Enhancing cooperation between all UN agencies and other private and government-sponsored health agencies.

6. Improving performance by constantly monitoring WHO's own efficiency and effectiveness.

World Health Organization

The more education this young girl in Nepal receives, the more opportunities will be open to her.

challenge the widespread tolerance and acceptance of violence against women are also important.

Make physical environments safer for women. Such measures should be

implemented **systematically**, by identifying places where violence against
women often occurs and analysing
why it occurs there. Depending on the
risk factors identified and the available resources, safety can be enhanced
through, for example, improving
lighting, increasing police and other
vigilance, particularly in areas where
alcohol or other drugs are consumed,
and opening up "blind spots" where an
assault could take place without anyone
being able to see or hear it happening.

Make schools safe for girls. Primary
and secondary school systems should be
heavily involved in making schools safe,
including **eradicating** teacher violence,
as well as engaging in broader anti-violence efforts. There is room for improve-
ment in action to eradicate physical
and sexual violence by teachers against
students in virtually all countries and
all schools. In some cases, this requires
fundamental changes within the education **sector**, and in school policies, environments and curricula. School policies
should prohibit the use of violence as a
form of punishment, and violence and
harassment by and between teachers
and students. Enforcement of such policies should be monitored. **Skills-based
education** is an effective way to enable

**systemati-
cally:**
involving
a system,
method, or
plan.

eradicating:
removing or
destroying
completely.

sector:
section.

**skills-based
education:**
teaching
focused on
necessary
skills.

students and staff to reduce potential conflicts, and to get involved in community actions to reduce violence and promote non-violent behaviour. School health programmes, such as HIV prevention programmes and reproductive health programmes (particularly those targeting sexually transmitted infections and unwanted pregnancies among adolescents) should address issues of

As doctors and nurses come in contact with women in need of treatment, they have opportunities to educate women about their rights.

gender, power, and freely given consent. To be effective, programmes should begin early, involve both girls and boys (although probably with different information and key messages, and with a balance of single-sex and mixed-sex discussions), and apply age-appropriate learning. Such programmes must also be supported by relevant school policies, a supportive school environment, and school health services or referrals to care for and counsel victims and witnesses of violent incidents and harassment.

Develop a comprehensive health sector response to the various impacts of violence against women. Many health providers see and treat (knowingly or not) millions of women living in violent relationships. Developing a **comprehensive** health sector response to the various impacts of violence against women is therefore vital, and action by specific health care services is also needed. At the planning level, this will require health officials to identify the sector's particular role within the wider **multisectoral** response, in **advocating** for prevention, and in providing services for women who have experienced violence. In particular, it is important to address the demonstrated reluctance of abused women to seek help. . . . These

comprehensive: extensive; covering a lot of information.

multisectoral: involving many sections.

advocating: speaking or writing in favor of; pleading on behalf of.

services need to contribute to empowering women in situations of violence, and to avoid over-medicalizing the problem. Health providers who see and care for abused women need to coordinate and work with other sectors, particularly the police and social services. This will require the creation of formal referral procedures and protocols. In addition to more general awareness-raising, the health sector needs to find ways to ensure that: (a) women who have experienced violence are not **stigmatized** or blamed when they seek help from health institutions, (b) women will receive appropriate medical attention and other assistance, and (c) their confidentiality and security will be ensured.

stigmatized:
set apart with a mark of disgrace.

Use reproductive health services as entry points for identifying and supporting women in abusive relationships, and for delivering referral or support services. The availability and widespread use of reproductive health services (including antenatal care, family planning services, post-abortion care and services dealing with sexually transmitted infections) in most countries give these services a potential advantage for identifying women in abusive relationships and offering them referrals or support services. . . . Recognizing that identification is not enough, **protocols** and referral systems need to be put in place to ensure that appropriate care, follow-up and support services are available. In settings where resources are limited and referral is not possible, health staff should at least be aware of the problem and should provide information about legal and counseling options, as well as supportive messages that emphasize that such violence is wrong, and that it is a widespread problem.

protocols: agreed upon standards and practices.

Strengthen formal and informal support systems for women living with violence. Since abused women are most likely to seek help from informal networks of friends, relatives and neighbours, strengthening these networks is important so that when women do reach out to friends and family, they are better able to respond in a sympathetic and supportive manner. Media activities highlighting the extent of violence and promoting the role of friends, neighbours, and relatives, as well as interventions to reduce the social stigma around violence may all help to reinforce **constructive** responses.

constructive: helpful for improving or advancing.

Sensitize legal and justice systems to the particular needs of women victims of violence. All those in the criminal

sensitized: made more sensitive to.

denigrating: criticizing; putting down.

justice systems (police, investigators, medico-legal staff, lawyers, judges, etc.) should be trained and **sensitized** to consider and address the particular needs and priorities of abused women, particularly those faced with violence by a partner or ex-partner. . . . Those administering the criminal justice system, especially police, should not undermine women complainants by taking the side or the perpetrator, or by disbelieving or **denigrating** complainants. Ideally there should be support for women bringing complaints.

Tara Smith, a woman who escaped a life of virtual slavery within a sex trafficking network, now works on behalf of women's rights around the world. She does not like to relive her past life, but she was willing to share her hopes for the future.

"The first step," she said, "is to name the problem. Come right out and admit it—this is *wrong*. It doesn't matter what our religion is, what our culture is, deep inside we all know it: it's wrong to treat another human being like an object. So once we've named the problem, we're shining a light on it, making it so governments and churches and individuals can no longer ignore it. And then we have to teach young people everywhere, in classrooms and in families, in casual conversations, in the media, and everywhere they turn: Human beings everywhere, no matter their color or their gender, their religion or their language, no matter what—they are all made in the image of God. So how can we treat each other with anything less than respect? We're all equal in the eyes of God. And the world will be safe for us all when we finally act as though we believe that."

Further Reading

Barnes, Virginia Lee. *Aman: The Story of a Somali Girl*. New York: Vintage, 2000.

Dirie, Waris. *Desert Flower*. New York: Harper, 2000.

———. *Desert Dawn*. London: Virago, 2002.

Kassinja, Fauziya. *Do They Hear You When You Cry?* New York: Delta, 2000.

McCormick, Patricia. *Sold*. New York: Hyperion, 2008.

Mortenson, Greg. *Three Cups of Tea: One Man's Mission to Promote Peace . . . One School at a Time*. New York: Penguin, 2007.

Nazer, Mende. *Slave*. New York: Public Affairs, 2004.

Souad. *Buried Alive: A Survivor of an "Honor Killing" Speaks Out*. New York: Grand Central, 2005.

For More Information

Female Genital Mutilation (WHO)
www.who.int/mediacentre/factsheets/
fs241/en/

Honor Killings (*National Geographic*)
news.nationalgeographic.com/
news/2002/02/0212_020212_honorkilling.
htm

Lotus Shoes
www.sfmuseum.org/chin/foot.html

Prostitution in America
abcnews.go.com/2020/story?id=4480892

Sex Slaves (Frontline)
www.pbs.org/wgbh/pages/frontline/
slaves/

Transgender Issues
www.apa.org/topics/transgender.htm

Women's History
www.nwhp.org/

Bibliography

Campbell, J. "Intimate Partner Violence and Physical Health Consequences. *Archives of Internal Medicine*, 2002, 162:1157–1163.

Campbell, J., C. Garcia-Moreno, and P. Sharps. "Abuse During Pregnancy in Industrialized and Developing Countries." *Violence Against Women*, 2004, 10:770–789.

Division for the Advancement of Women, *Violence Against Women: A Statistical Overview, Challenges and Gaps in Data Collection and Methodology and Approaches for Overcoming Them*. Geneva, Switzerland: April 11–14, 2005. www.un.org/womenwatch/daw/egm/vaw-stat-2005.

Egan, Shannon. "Sexual Violence Threatens Women and Girls in Kenya's Post-Election Crisis." UNFPA. March 5, 2008. www.unfpa.org/news/news.cfm?ID=1102.

Human Rights Watch. "The Police Should Protect Us, Not Beat Us." May 2008. hrw.org/reports/2008/turkey0508/6.htm.

———. "Sexual Orientation, Gender Identity, and the Law in Kyrgyzstan." October 2008. www.hrw.org/reports/2008/kyrgyzstan1008/4.htm.

Jansen, H. "Interviewer Training in the WHO Multi-Country Study on Women's Health and Domestic Violence." *Violence Against Women*, 10:831–849, 2004.

Bibliography

Jewkes, R., P. Sen, and C. Garcia-Moreno. "Sexual Violence." In E. G. Krug, ed. *World Report on Violence and Health*. Geneva: World Health Organization, 2002.

Johnson, M. "Conflict and Control: Images of Symmetry and Asymmetry in Domestic Violence." In A. Booth, A. Crouter, and M. Clements, eds. *Couples in Conflict*. Hillsdale, N.J.: Lawrence Erlbaum, 2000.

Krug, E.G., ed. *World Report on Violence and Health*. Geneva, Switzerland: World Health Organization, 2002.

Mayell, Hilary. "Thousands of Women Killed for Family 'Honor'." *National Geographic News*, February 12, 2002. news.nationalgeographic.com/news/2002/02/0212_020212_honorkilling.html.

Niles, Chris. "Report Reveals Kenyan Child Sex Industry of 'Horrific' Magnitude. UNICEF. www.unicef.org/infobycountry/kenya_37817.html.

PlusNews: Global HIV/AIDS News and Analysis. "Kenya: Young Girls the New Bait for Fishermen." Sept. 12, 2008. www.plusnews.org/Report.aspx?ReportId=80315.

———. "Kenya: Emily Ajwang': 'When You Have Children, You Will Do Anything to Feed Them." Oct. 3, 2008. www.plusnews.org/Report.aspx?ReportId=80735.

Bibliography

Sittoni, Pamella. "Sex Tourism in Kenya: One Girl's Story." UNICEF. Dec. 20, 2006. www. unicef.org/infobycountry/kenya_37823.html.

Tady, Megan. "Transgender People Face Obstacles, Violence." *The New Standard*. July 15, 2007. newstandardnews.net/content/ index.cfm/items/4103.

Tjaden P. and N. Thoennes. Extent, Nature and *Consequences of Intimate Partner Violence: Findings from the National Violence Against Women Survey*. Washington, D.C.: National Institute of Justice, Centers for Disease Control and Prevention, 2000.

UNICEF. "Gender Discrimination and Inequalities Across Regions." www.unicef.org/ sowc07/docs/sows07_1_2.pdf.

United Nations. *United Nations Millennium Declaration*. General Assembly Resolution, 55th session, document A/RES/55/2, Chapter III, number 11, September 2000.

U.S. Department of Health and Human Services. "Female Genital Cutting." womenshealth.gov/faq/fgc.htm.

Wang, Sheng. "Female Genital Mutilation." MedHunters.com. http://www.medhunters. com/articles/fgm.html.

Bibliography

"War Against Women." www.cbsnews.com/stories/2008/01/11/60minutes/main3701249.shtml.

Watts, C. Putting Women First: Ethical and *Safety Recommendations for Research on Domestic Violence Against Women*. Geneva: World Health Organization, 2001. (document WHO/EIP/GPE/01.1, available at whqlibdoc.who.int/hq/2001/WHO_FCH_GWH_01.1.pdf).

Women's International Center. "Women's History in America." http://www.wic.org/misc/history.htm.

World Health Organization. "Gender, Women, and Health." www.who.int/gender/whatisgender/en/.

———. *Handbook for the Documentation of Interpersonal Violence Prevention Programmes*. Geneva: World Health Organization, 2004.

———. *WHO Multi-Country Study on Women's Health and Domestic Violence Against Women*. Geneva, Switzerland: World Health Organization, 2005.

El Universal (The Universal Newspaper). January 10, 2003.

Index

abuse 37, 92, 115–118
  emotional abuse 36, 37
attitude 17, 29, 30, 50, 65, 88

bias 26

Christian 15–17, 55, 57, 79, 88
common law 21, 22
culture 9, 10, 14, 15, 17, 21, 28, 73, 76, 77, 81, 83, 92, 103, 105, 107, 109, 118

discrimination 23, 26, 29, 30, 32, 81, 84, 88

economic 26, 28, 31, 49, 54, 61, 79
education 19–21, 26–28, 30, 33, 53, 57, 59, 110, 112, 113
employment 24, 29, 33, 110

female 9, 11, 12, 17, 27, 28, 76, 77, 79, 80, 83, 86
  genital cutting (FGC) 76–81
feminine 9, 12, 14, 15, 17, 20, 32, 73, 83, 85, 86
foot binding 73, 75–77

gender 9–14, 17, 20, 24, 26, 29–34, 39, 44, 50, 53, 80, 81, 83, 85, 87, 88, 90–93, 110, 115, 119
  gender discrimination 23, 26, 29, 30, 32, 81, 84, 88
  Gender Empowerment Measure (GEM) 31, 32
  gender expectations 18, 19, 21, 24, 26

gender identity 9, 14, 22, 76, 80, 83, 87, 89, 97
gender limitations 18, 22
gender roles 12, 17, 20, 24, 26, 83
transgender 83–92

honor killings 34, 104–106

kidnap 61, 63, 64

legal 19, 21, 22, 24, 29, 33, 43, 88, 106, 110, 117, 118
  protection 24, 43

male 9, 11, 12, 17, 23, 27, 29, 30, 53, 73, 79, 83–86, 88
masculine 9, 12, 15, 32, 83, 86

political 23, 30, 31, 39, 41, 42, 44, 47
prejudice 29, 30, 84
prostitute 23, 49, 52, 55–57, 59, 61, 62

religion 29, 79, 90, 93, 107, 118, 119

sex trafficking 61, 63–65, 118
sexual assault 40, 43
  rape 36, 39, 43, 44, 45, 61, 99, 106
sexually transmitted diseases 44, 114
slavery 55, 60, 63, 118
society 10, 14, 17, 19, 30, 31, 50, 84, 109
socioeconomic 110, 116
  HIV/AIDS 36, 47, 49, 52–55, 59, 80, 114

Index

UNICEF 59, 50, 105
United Nations (UN) 31, 40, 80, 105, 107, 109

victims 61, 63, 87, 88, 106, 115, 117
violence 33–36, 39, 40, 45, 47, 80, 84, 87, 88, 91, 92, 105, 109, 110, 112–118

domestic violence 33, 110
sexual violence 39, 40, 43, 113

World Health Organization (WHO) 9, 32, 33, 36, 37, 110

Picture Credits

About the Authors and the Consultant

Authors

Rae Simons has written many books for young adults. She lives in New York State with her teenage children.

Joyce Zoldak lives in New York City and works for the nonprofit sector. She will be pursuing a master's degree in Urban Policy in fall 2009.

Consultant

Andrew M. Kleiman, M.D. is a Clinical Instructor in Psychiatry at New York University School of Medicine. He received a BA in philosophy from the University of Michigan, and graduated from Tulane University School of Medicine. Dr. Kleiman completed his internship, residency, and fellowship in psychiatry at New York University and Bellevue Hospital. He is currently in private practice in Manhattan and teaches at New York University School of Medicine.